What are Thinkologie Books?

Thinkologie Books are a product of over 20 years of teaching the languages of

Hindi and American English.

Our books focus on teaching language through puzzles, games, or stories!

People love stories! Which is why we like to teach language in the cultural

context. Each book is interactive with activities to test comprehension.

The stories are non-fiction based on famous biographies, tales, and legends.

The content of each book is conceived, adapted, and written by

Nicole Herbert Dean.

AI generates the illustrations of some books.

Copyright 2023 Nicole Herbert Dean

Trace the alphabet in the
following pages

अ a आ aa इ e ई ee

उ o ऊ oo ए ay ऐ aay

ओ o औ au ऋ ri अं um अः uh

क, ख, ग, घ, ड़,

च, छ, ज, झ, अ,

ट, ठ, ड, ढ, ण,

त, थ, द, ध, न,

प, फ, ब, भ, म,

य, र, ल, व, श,

ष, स, ह

Color the fruit
and then write and
pronounce their names

Apple – सेब (Seb)

Banana - केला (Kela)

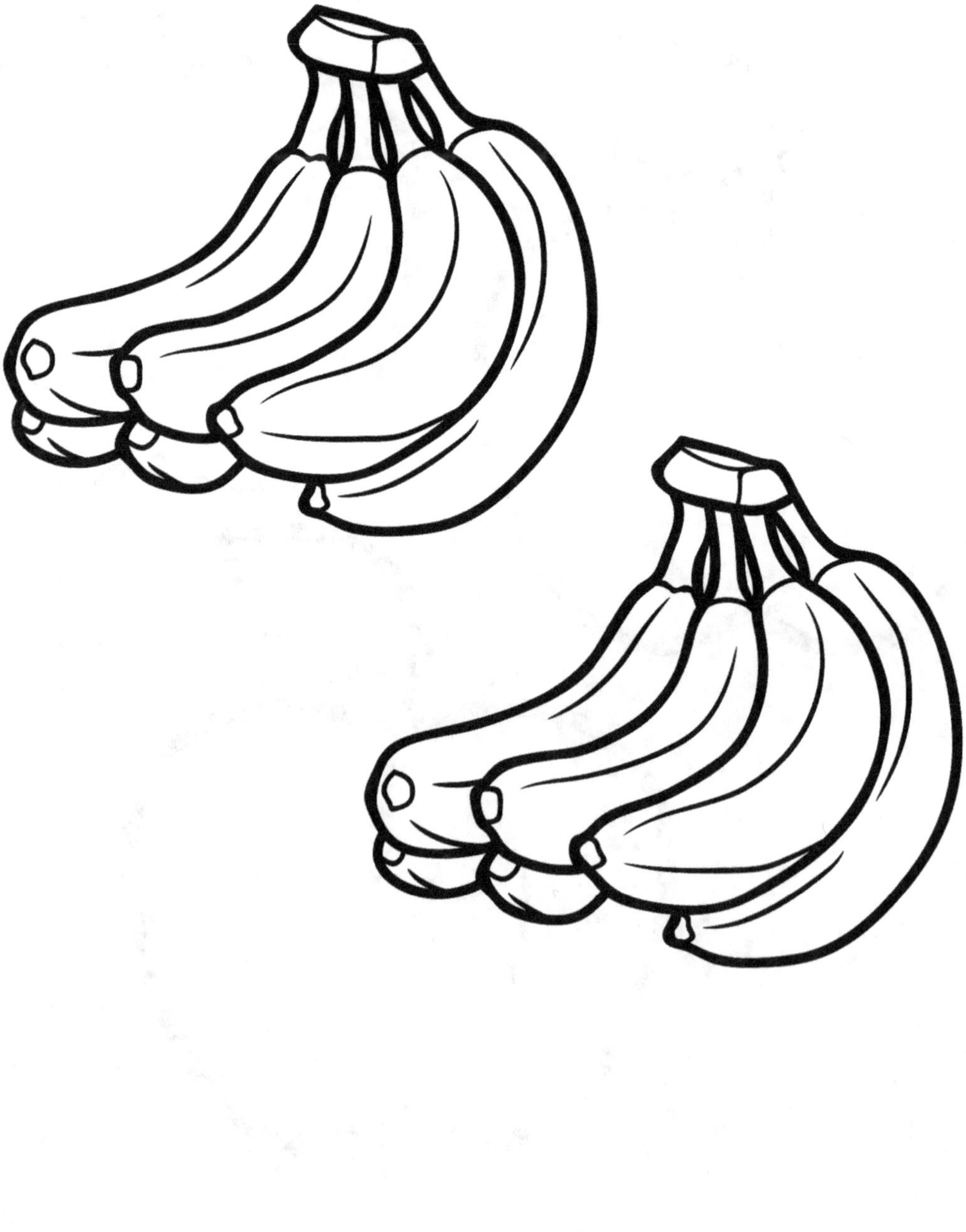

Mango – आम (Aam)

Orange – संतरा (Santra)

Grapes – अंगूर (Angoor)

Pineapple - अनानास (Ananas)

Watermelon – तरबूज (Tarbuj)

Papaya – पपीता (Papita)

Guava – अमरूद (Amrud)

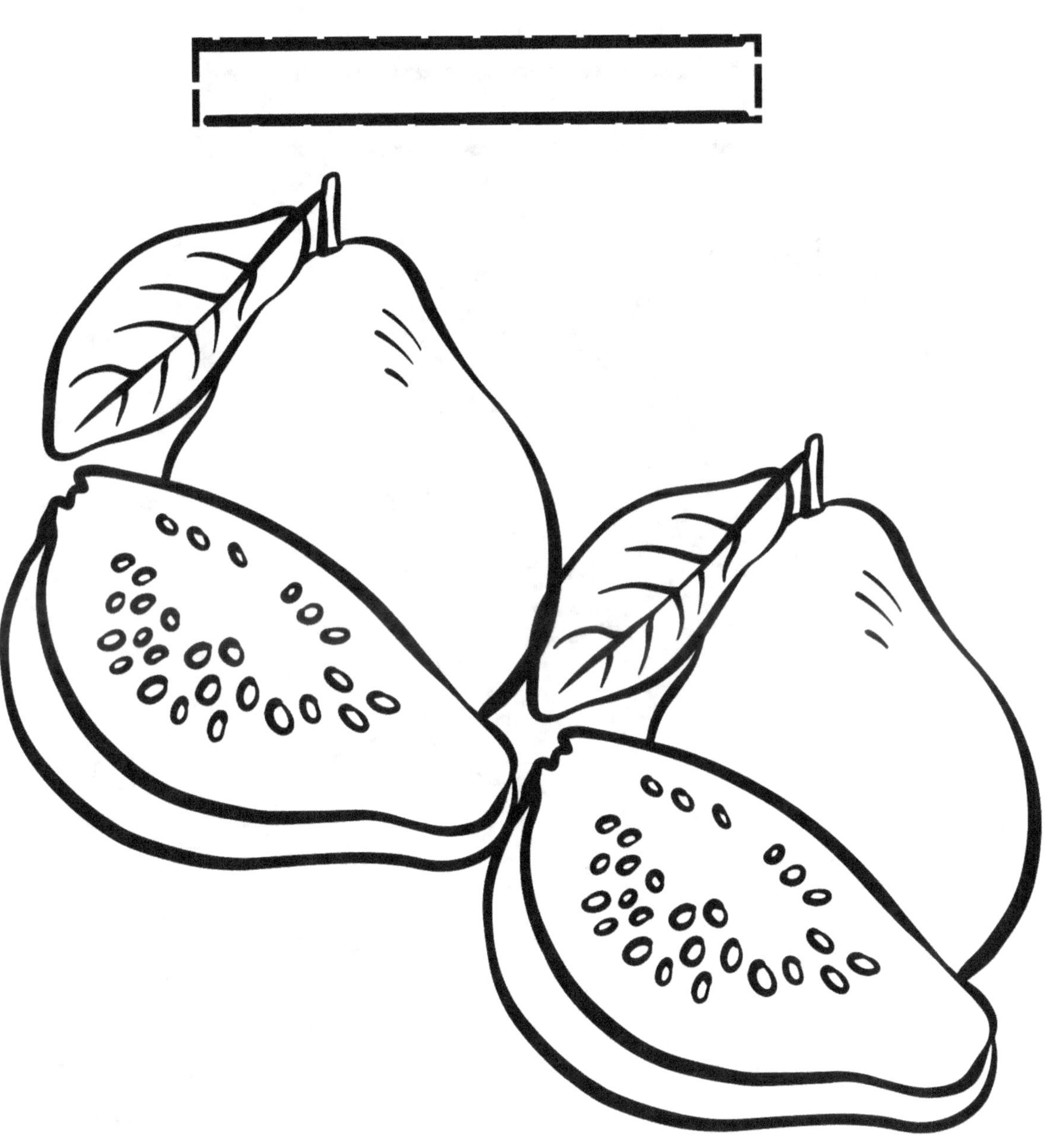

Pomegranate – अनार (Anar)

Practice the numbers
Trace and pronounce each word

शून्य shoonya

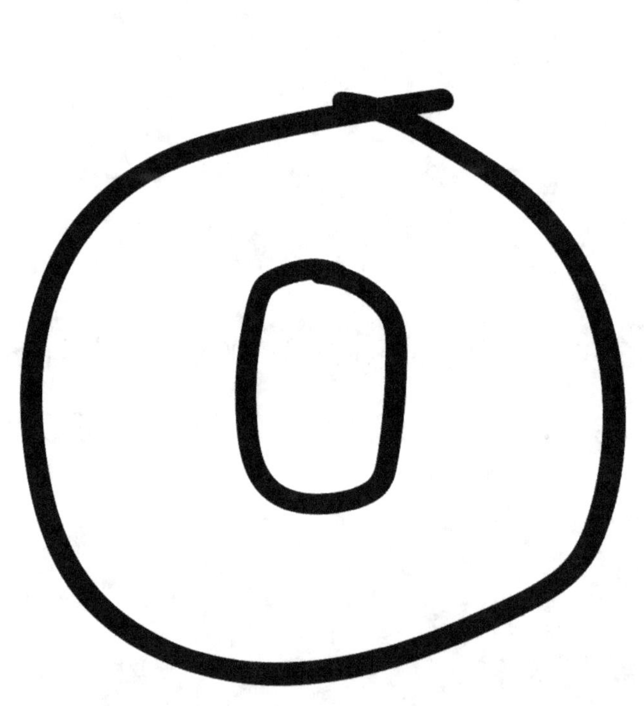

एक ek

दो dhough

तीन teen

चार char

पाँच paanch

ਛਹ chuh

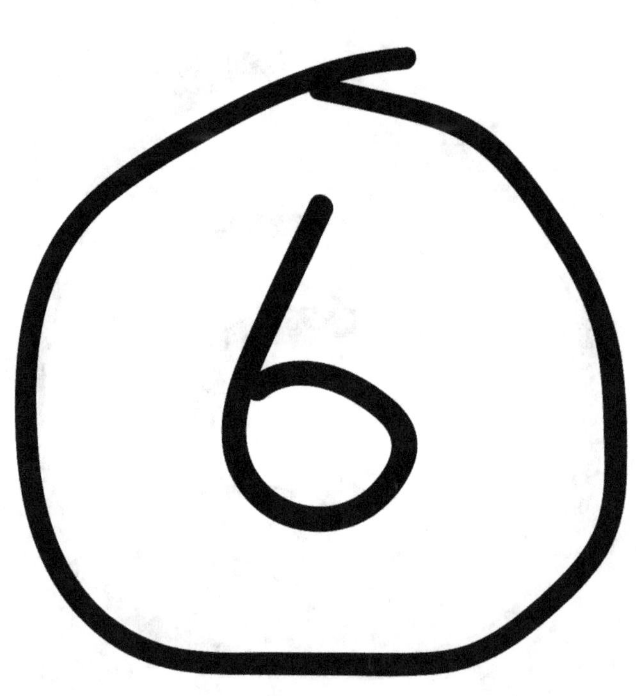

सात saat

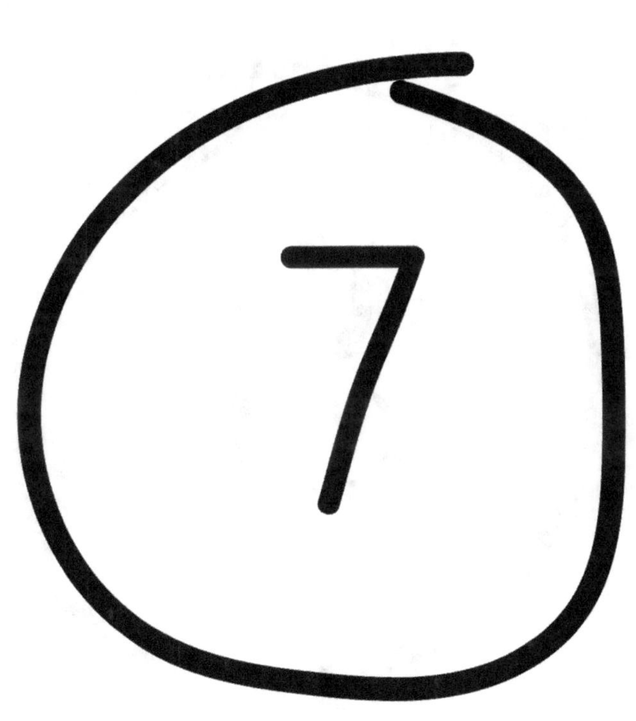

आठ aat

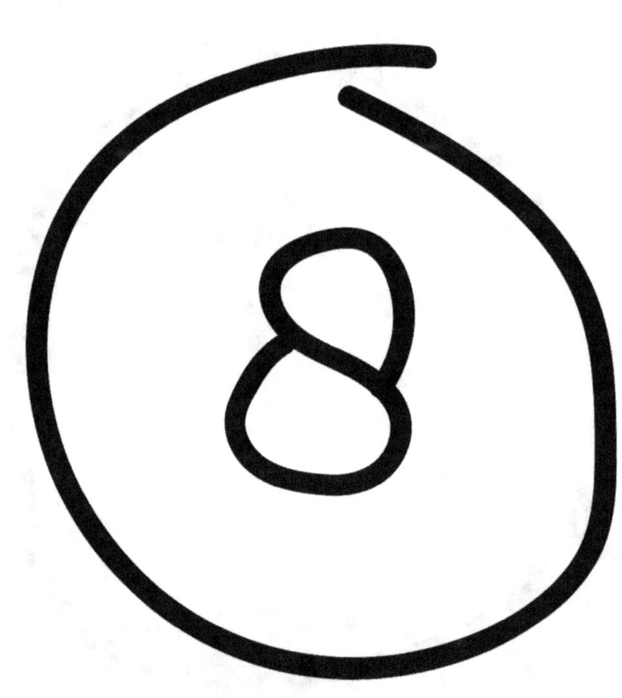

नौ nau

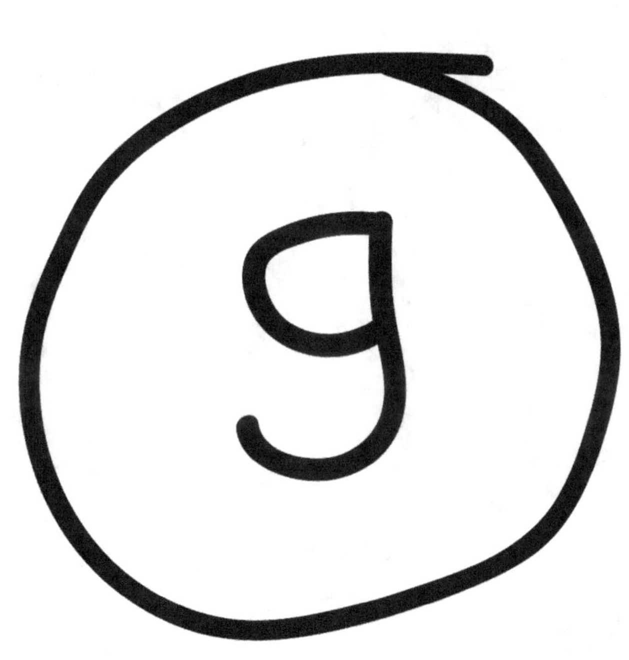

दस dus

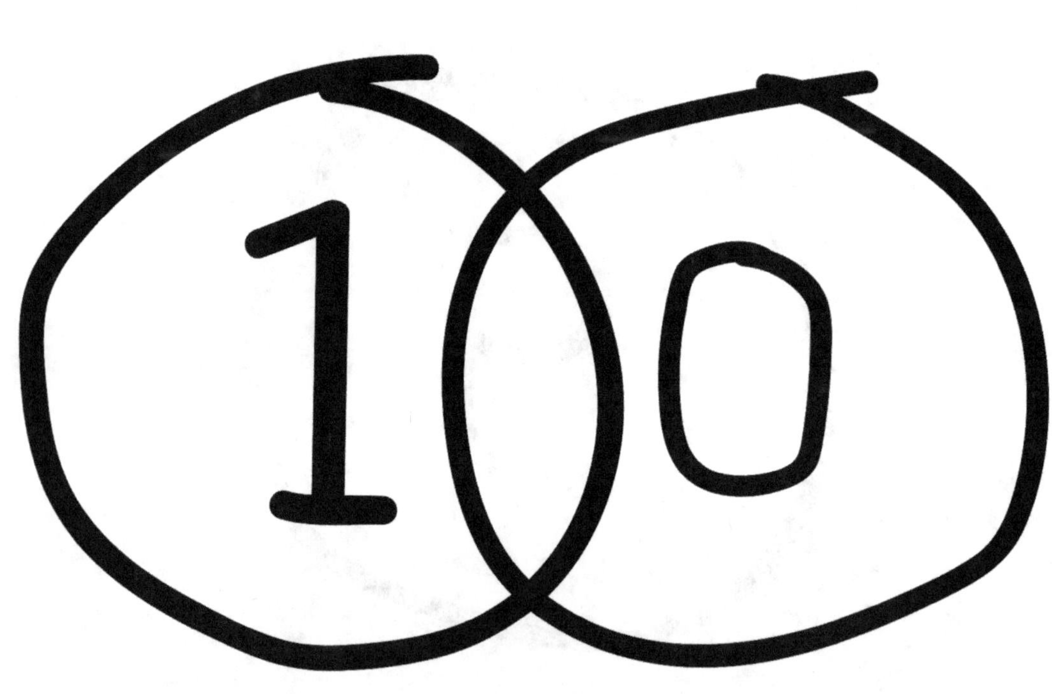

color the creatures
and
pronounce the words

ant
चींटी cheentee

bee
मधुमक्खी madhumakhi

cow
गाय guy

dog
कुत्ता kuttha

elephant
हाथी haathee

frog
मेंढक mendhak

giraffe
जिराफ giraaf

horse
घोड़ा ghoda

iguana
गोधा godha

jackal

सियार siyaar

koala bear
कोअला भालू koala
bhaloo

lion
सिंह sinh

monkey
बंदर bandar

nightingale
बुलबुल bulbul

owl
उल्लू ulloo

parrot
तोता thotha

quail
बटेर bater

rabbit
खरगोश khargosh

squirrel
गिलहरी gilhari

tiger
बाघ **bagh**

unicorn fish
गेंडा मछली genda machlee

vampire bat
चमगादड़ chamagaadadd

wolf
भेड़िया bhediya

xray fish
एक्स रे मछली xray machlee

yak
याक **yaak**

zebra

बनैला गधा **bunnayla gadha**

Color the pictures
and
pronounce the words

blizzard
बर्फानी तूफान barafaani toofan

cloudy
धुंधला dhoondhla

drought
सूखा sookha

flood
बाढ़ baadd

foggy
धूमिल dhoomil

hail
ओले ole

rain

वर्षा **varsha**

snowy
हिमाच्छन्न himacchann

sunny
धूप dhoop

thunderstorm
आंधी तूफान aandhee toofan

windy
तूफानी toofanee

Rainbow
इंद्रधनुष indradhanush

Color the shapes
and pronounce the words

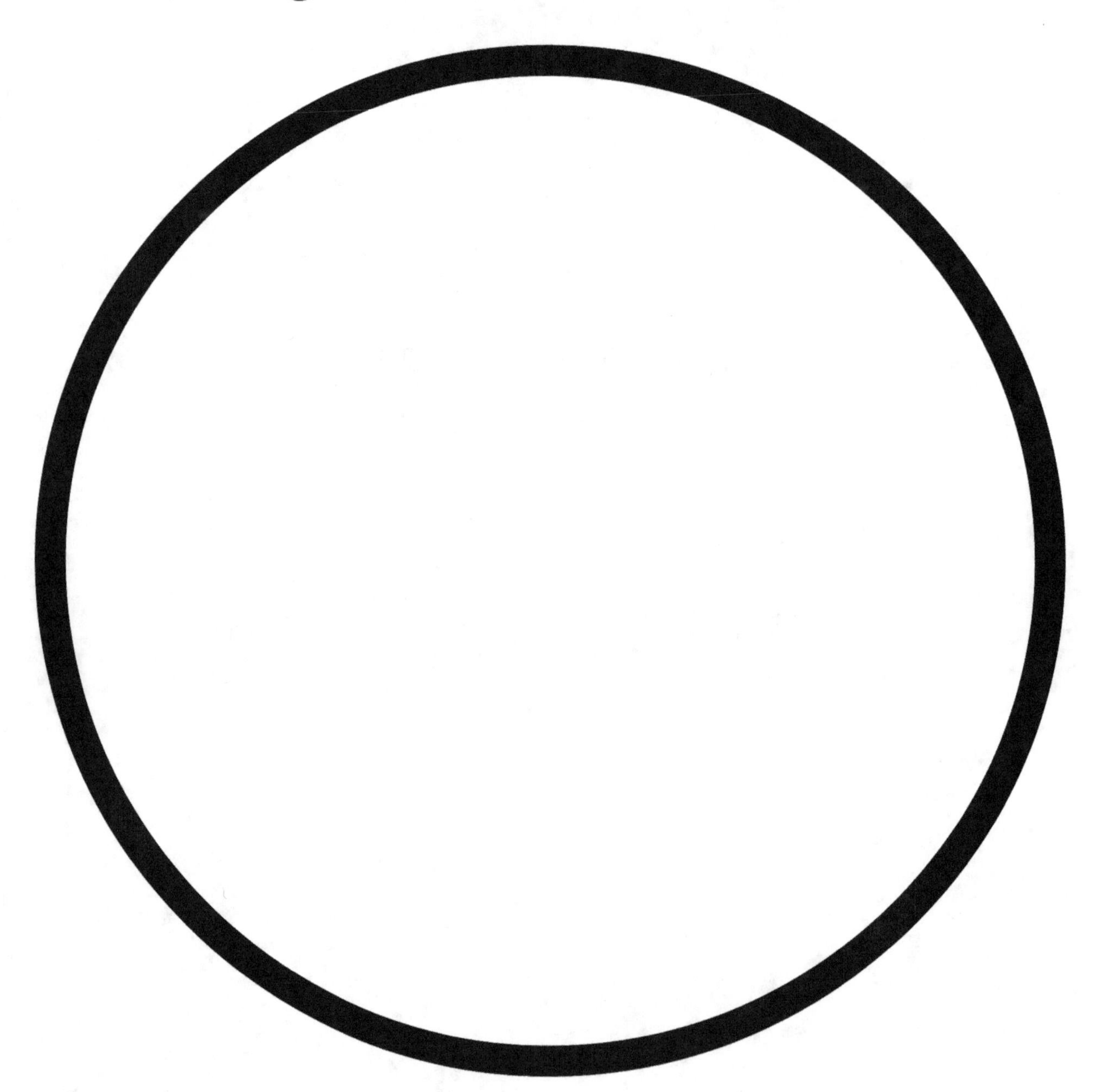

color the circle red
लाल laal = red
वृत्त vrut = circle
लाल

color the rectangle blue

आयत aayat= rectangle

नीला neela = blue

color the square yellow

वर्ग varg = square

पीला peela = yellow

color the triangle green

त्रिकोण trikoan = triangle

हरा hara = green

color the hexagon purple

षट्भुज shatbhuj = hexagon

बैंगनी baigani = purple

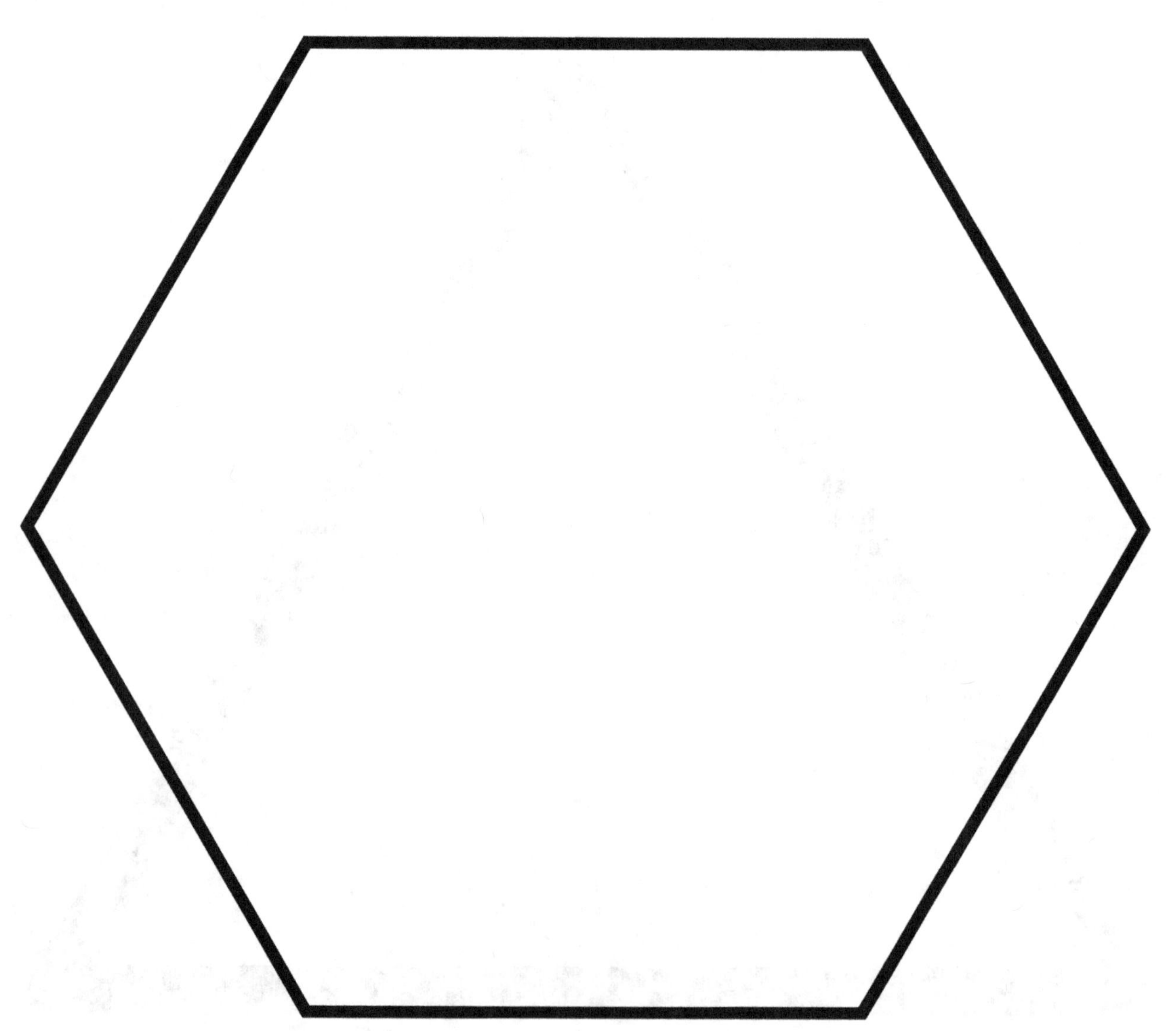

color the heart red

दिल dil = heart

लाल laal = red

color the pentagon pink

पंचकोण panchkoan = pentagon

गुलाबी gulabi = pink

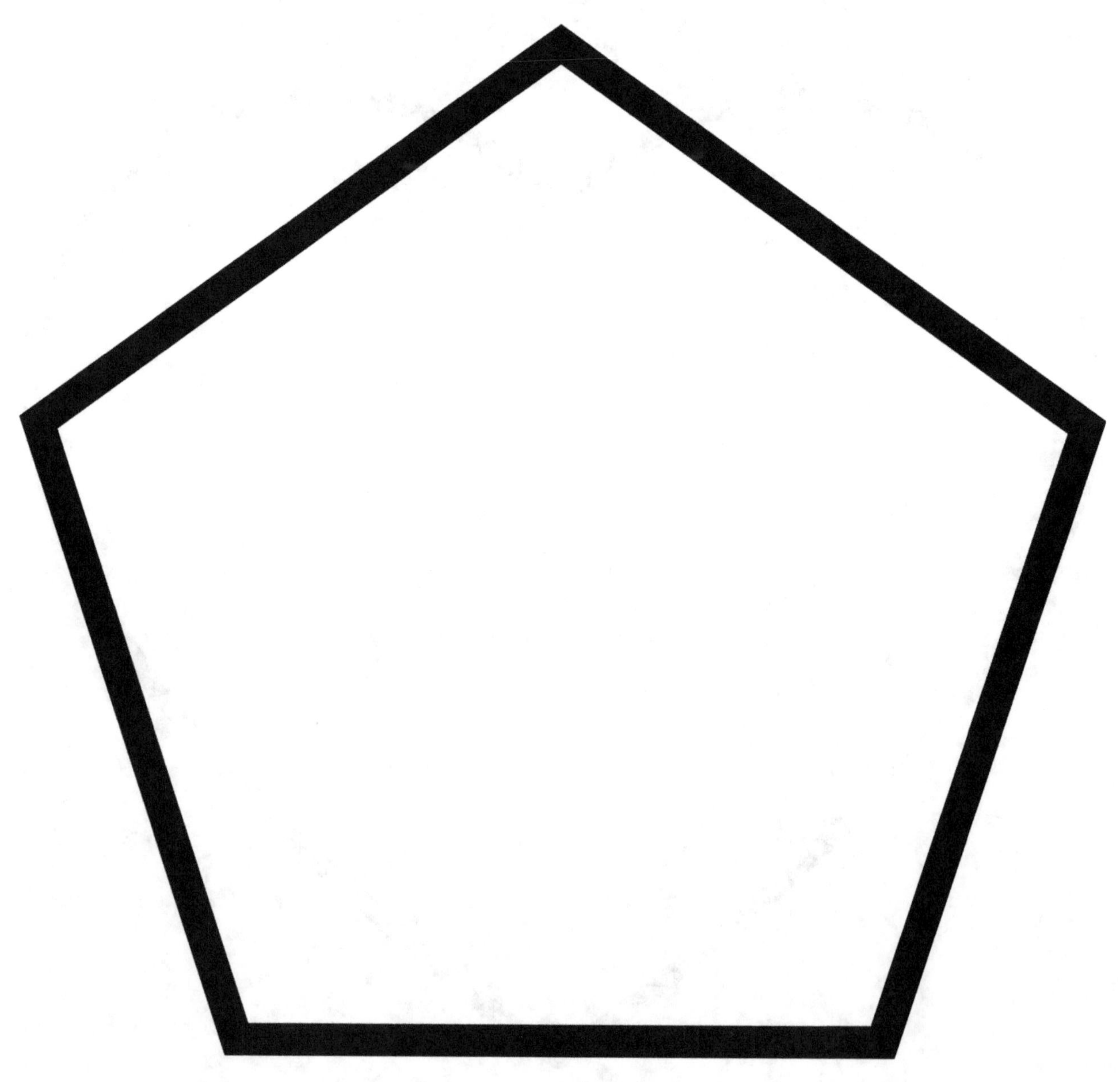

color the star greyy

सितारा sitara = star

स्लेटी slatee = grey

color the diamond orange
हीरा heera = diamond
नारंगी naarangee = orange

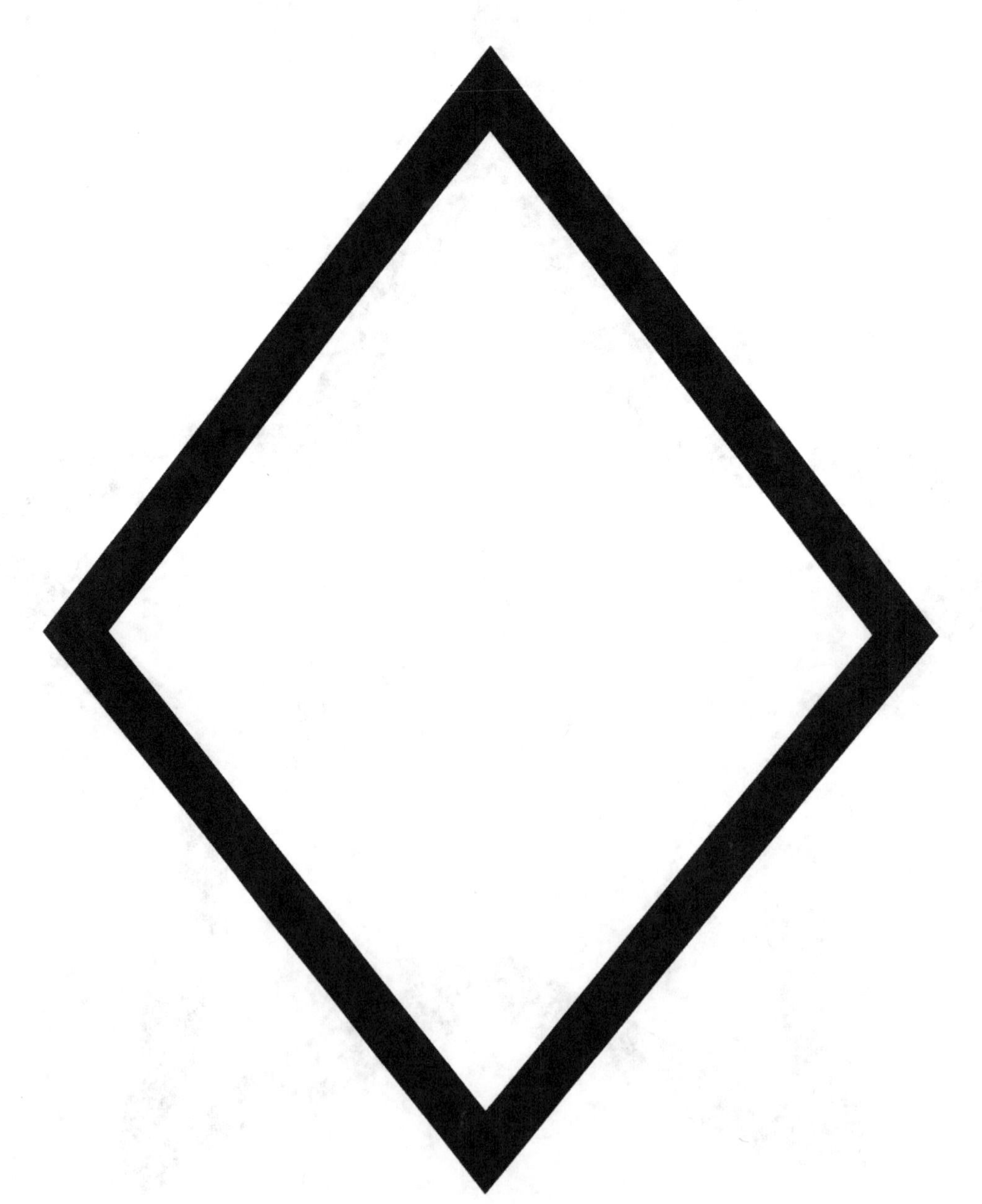

Write out the parts of the body

बाल baal

माथा *maathaa*

____
____

कान kaan

भौहें bhowhain

आँख aankh

नाक **naak**

____

____

जीभ *jeeb*

दाँत daanth

ठुड्डी tooddee

CHIN

गरदन gardun

___

कंधे **kandhay**

छाती chaathee

CHEST

पेट payt

____

____

बांह **banh**

उंगलियां oongliyaan

नितंब nitamb

पैर *pair*

घुटने ghutnay

एड़ी edee

पैर की अंगुली
pair ki ungooli

Practice each verb
write it out
pronounce as you write

to be – होना (hona)

do – करना (karna)

say – कहना (kehna)

get (obtain) – पाना (pana)

go – जाना (jana)

know - जानना (janna)

take – लेना (lena)

see - देखना (dekhna)

come – आना (ana)

think – सोचना (sochna)

look - देखना (dekhna)

want - चाहना (chahna)

give – देना (dena)

use – इस्तेमाल करना
(istemal karna)

find – ढूँढना (dhundhna)

tell – बताना (batana)

ask – पूछना (puchna)

work – काम करना
(kam karna)

seem - लगना (lagna)

feel – महसूस करना (mahsus karna)

Practice writing the words

जागो
jaago
wake up

Practice writing the Hindi words below

घर आओ
ghar aao
come home

Practice writing the Hindi words below

किताब पढो
kitaab pado
read the book

Practice writing the Hindi words below

स्कूल जाओ
school jaao
go to school

Practice writing the Hindi words below

नाश्ता खाओ
nashta khao
eat breakfast

Practice writing the Hindi words below

स्नान करो

snaan karo

take a shower

Practice writing the Hindi words below

दाँतों को साफ करो
danto ko saaf karo
brush your teeth

Practice writing the Hindi words below

Contact us

Our mission is to help other educators, coaches, and homeschoolers also!

Contact us for customized interactive books. If you want to publish your course into a book - contact us!

Our website:

www.thinkologie.co

Follow our author page

https://amazon.com/author/thinkologiebooks

We are also on:

Instagram @thinkologie

Twitter @thinkologie

Facebook @thinkologiemedia

सो जाओ
so jaao
go to sleep

Practice writing the Hindi words below

खाना खाओ
khana khao
eat dinner

Practice writing the Hindi words below

पढ़ाई करो
padaee karo
do your homework

Practice writing the Hindi words below